NATURE WATCH

TIDE POOLS
LIFE AT THE EDGE OF THE SEA

Revised Edition

Anita Malnig

Lerner Publications Company • Minneapolis

CONTENTS

For my parents, Lawrence and Laura Malnig, who introduced me to the sea

Consulting Editor: Franklin H. Barnwell, Professor, Department of Ecology, Evolution, and Behavior, University of Minnesota

Lerner Publications Company
A division of Lerner Publishing Group, Inc.
241 First Avenue North
Minneapolis, MN 55401 U.S.A.

Website address: www.lernerbooks.com

Library of Congress Cataloging-in-Publication Data

Malnig, Anita.
   Tide pools : life at the edge of the sea / by Anita Malnig. — Rev. ed.
     p.   cm. — (Nature watch)
   Rev. ed. of: Where the waves break / by Anita Malnig. ©1985.
   Includes bibliographical references and index.
   ISBN 978-1-58013-945-8 (lib. bdg : alk. paper)
   1. Seashore biology—Juvenile literature. I. Malnig, Anita. Where the waves break. II. Title.
QH95.7.M347 2009
578.769'9—dc22   2008029075

Manufactured in the United States of America
1 2 3 4 5 6 - DP - 14 13 12 11 10 09

The coast of Maui, Hawaii

TIDES AND
TIDE POOLS

THE EDGE OF THE SEA IS A CURIOUS PLACE. WHETHER THE coastline is rocky or sandy, life at the seashore brews and bubbles, but seeing it often takes a sharp eye. Whole neighborhoods of sea creatures may live under the rocks or burrowed in the sand. Some sneak out for food at night, dodging larger animals. Others never leave their damp, dark hiding places. Still other animals are in disguise, looking more like plants than animals. The closer you look, the more you will see.

If you go to the beach at different times of the day, you will notice that the shore looks different. Sometimes the water comes far up on the shore, covering rock and beach. This is called **high tide**. At other times, you can walk far out on the beach, over the area that was covered by water during high tide. This is **low tide**. Low tide is a good time to look for shells and rocks or for animals that live in the sand.

The moon has a lot to do with these high and low **tides**. Like Earth, the moon has a gravitational pull. The moon's gravitational pull makes the water that is nearest to the moon rise up. The water on the opposite side of Earth also piles up higher, but this rise is caused largely by the rotation, or spinning, of Earth. This means that two places are always having a high tide at the same time. And two other places are having a low tide at the same time.

Low tide comes 6 hours and about 13 minutes after high tide. Then the day's second high tide comes, 12 hours and 25 minutes after the first. The following day, the two high tides and the two low tides will happen 50 minutes later than they had the day before.

During low tide, we can wander far out along the beach and see plants and animals that at another time might be underwater. One very good place to look is in a **tide pool**. A tide pool is just that—a small pool filled with ocean water that was left behind when the tide went out. You'll find these pools mostly on rocky coasts where the rocks make holes that collect the water.

Low tide reveals tide pools covering a beach in California.

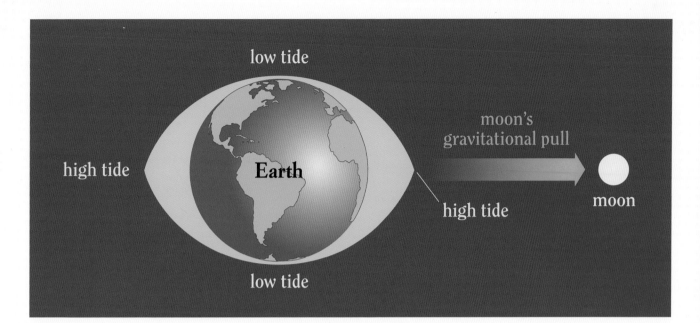

low tide

moon's
gravitational pull

high tide

Earth

high tide

moon

low tide

High tide at the same beach in California

Colorful plants cover these rocks on a Washington beach. Tide pools have also formed near the rocks.

Each pool is its own little community. Sea creatures you find in one may not be in another. Tide pool life varies according to location and climate as well. You would not expect to find exactly the same animals in a New England tide pool as you would in a Mediterranean one. Some kinds of tide pool creatures exist almost anywhere in the world—starfish, sponges, and mussels, to name just a few—even though their colors, sizes, and shapes may vary from place to place.

Sometimes during low tide, the pools dry out a little. This can be a problem for the creatures living there. Some hide from the sun under rocks where it is damp and dark. Others hide in clumps of seaweed.

Tide Pool Species Zones

gulls

spray zone

periwinkle snails

turban snails

high tide zone

mussels

starfish

hermit crabs

clams

low tide zone

starfish

sea urchins

clams

submerged zone

sponge

sand dollar

seaweed

sponge

brittle star

sea cucumber

seaweed

This diagram shows where tide pool species often live. Animals in the spray zone are almost always uncovered. Those in the high tide zone are underwater only during high tide. As the tide goes out, those in the low tide zone become uncovered. Species in the submerged zone are always underwater.

Above: These turban snails live in a tide pool in California. The black outer layer of some shells has worn off. *Opposite page:* A common periwinkle eats off the seafloor.

SHELLED TIDE POOL DWELLERS

SOME ANIMALS THAT MAKE THEIR HOMES IN TIDE POOLS belong to a group called **mollusks**. Mollusks can be very different from one another. But most have soft, boneless bodies and a hard outer shell. Some mollusks thrive in deeper parts of the ocean. Others, however, live better at the water's edge or even on land.

SNAILS

The snail is one type of mollusk you're very likely to find in or around a tide pool. There are about 40,000 different kinds of saltwater snails, and there are many others that live in freshwater or on land.

A snail often looks as if it is slowly sliding along, but it is using its foot to get around. A snail has one muscular foot. The snail squeezes its foot muscles together and then lets them go, inching along bit by bit.

The underside of a black turban snail shows the snail's mouth, foot, and feelers.

Some snails use their feet as shovels. A tiny digging action moves what is in the snail's path and helps the snail go forward. **Burrowing**—digging a tunnel and then using it for shelter—comes in handy if a snail needs to escape from another animal, like a starfish. There is even one kind of snail, called a harp shell, that can use its foot to trick animals wanting to capture it. This snail is able to break off the back part of its foot. That broken-off part remains wriggling in the sand, sure to attract the attention of the attacking animal. Meanwhile, the rest of the snail can sneak off.

Snails also have one or two pairs of tentacles that help them sense danger. On one pair, often at the tips, are the snail's eyes.

You'll find snails in ocean waters all over the world. Adult snails range in length from .04 inches (1 mm) to 2 feet (60 cm) or more. These 2-foot-long snails live in waters around Australia. The longest snail of all is almost 52 inches (132 cm) long and makes itself at home in the body of a sea cucumber. Though unusually long, this snail is only 0.2 inches (5 mm) in diameter.

The periwinkle, a common tide pool snail, is easy to find. Periwinkles cluster together by the hundreds on rocks, many in cracks and crevices. A filmy layer of **algae**, a plant-like growth, covers the rocks, but you may not be able to see it. Using teeth too small to see, the periwinkle grazes these algae for its daily food.

As many as 860 million periwinkles can live along just 1 mile (1.6 km) of rocky coast. Together in one year they can eat about 2,200 tons (2,000 metric tons) of material, but only 55 tons (50 metric tons) is food they can digest. The rest is the rock they scraped off along with the algae!

Periwinkles attached to an algae-covered rock in the United Kingdom

CLAMS

You'll find clams on the bottom of the ocean in either shallow or deep water or buried in the sand along the beach when the tide is out. Clams are **bivalves**, as are oysters, mussels, and scallops. Bivalves are creatures that have two shells hinged together in one place. Different varieties of clams live all over the world.

Water enters and leaves the clam's shells through a pair of tubes called **siphons**. The siphons stick out of the shells when the water around the clam is high. Water and food particles of plants and animals can then flow into the clam. But when the tide is out or at any time the clam senses danger, it pulls in its siphons—and its foot—and fastens its shells tightly closed. This is where we get the expression "clamming up."

Clams have two shells that open and close. This clam is digging into an Oregon beach.

Two wart-necked piddock clams are burrowed into the seafloor off the coast of California. Their siphons stretch up to allow the clam to breathe and eat.

A clam's foot can extend downward through the open shells. The clam is able to dig deeply into sand or mud with this foot. In this way, it can hide from creatures that might want to turn it into a meal.

This surf clam has its foot sticking out as it begins to bury itself.

At low tide, this California beach is covered with bean clams.

Above: Low tide uncovers ochre sea stars on a rock face on the coast of British Columbia, Canada. Ochre sea stars can be three colors—orange *(opposite page)*, brown, and purple.

STARS, SPINES, AND SEA CUCUMBERS

ANOTHER GROUP OF TIDE POOL DWELLERS IS KNOWN FOR having spiny skin. These animals also have tube feet and often have a five-point body shape (like a star). They are called **echinoderms**. These spiny creatures are at home all along the ocean bottom—including tide pools in coastal areas.

STARFISH

You'll find starfish on the rocks or in the water of tide pools or in sandy puddles on the beach, just about all over the world. The starfish gets its name because its arms, also called **rays**, often make it look like a star. Along those arms, the starfish has little **tube feet** tipped with suction cups. These can grasp rocks tightly and are used by the starfish to move around. At the end of each arm is a light-sensitive **eyespot**. This eyespot

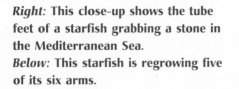

cannot see things, but it can tell light from dark.

Some starfish may throw off parts of their arms if they are disturbed. New arms will grow in about a year.

The starfish's mouth is in the middle of the underside of its body. With its arms, it can pull at the shells of bivalves like clams and mussels. When a clam's shells open

just the tiniest bit, the starfish pushes its stomach out of its mouth and into the bivalve. Now the stomach is inside out and can begin to digest the clam meat while outside of the starfish's body.

Starfish lay their eggs in water. The eggs have developed inside of the starfish's arms and come out of tiny holes on the upper sides, near the bases of the arms.

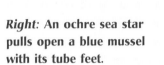

Right: An ochre sea star pulls open a blue mussel with its tube feet.

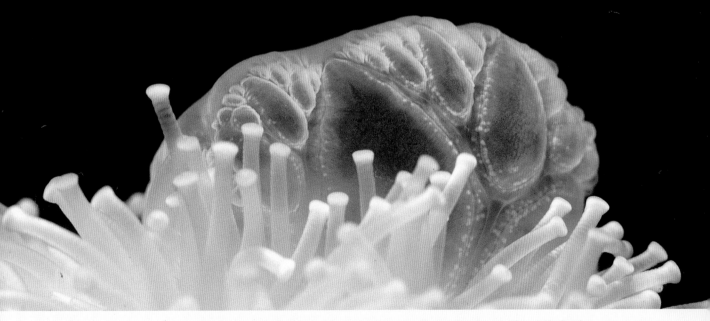

Above: A starfish's stomach is extended beyond its tube feet to digest food outside of its body.

BRITTLE STARS

Brittle stars are similar to starfish, their cousins. They get their name from the ease with which they break off arms. As with starfish, brittle star arms grow back. Their arms, however, are usually longer and more flexible than those of starfish, helping them to move faster.

Sometimes the brittle star slithers along by stretching an arm forward, fixing the tip of it to a surface, and then pulling its body forward by wriggling and bending the stretched-out arm. The brittle star can also crawl about in two other ways. One arm can lead, two can trail behind, and the two in between can move in a rowing or pushing motion. Or four arms can row and the fifth will trail behind.

This is the underside of a brittle star. It is regrowing one of its arms.

Sponge brittle stars, such as this one found in the Caribbean Sea, live mainly on sponges. Brittle stars and sponges live in submerged zones of tide pools.

The tube feet on a brittle star's arms usually don't have suction cups. They are used to breathe, to feel around, and to "sniff" out the small living and dead animals that brittle stars like to eat.

You can find brittle stars in all the oceans of the world. Some live in deep water and some in shallow water, including tide pools. You'll never find brittle stars on the rocks above the water, though. They need to be in water all the time.

Green sea urchins underwater

SEA URCHINS

The colorful, prickly sea urchin can anchor itself to rocks with its spines and tube feet so that the waves won't wash it away. As it holds on tight, it gnaws part of the rock away with its teeth. The sea urchin's mouth, located on the underside of its body, has five powerful white teeth and looks so much like an ancient Greek oil lantern that it has been called Aristotle's Lantern.

This relative of the starfish and brittle star is covered with spines more prominent than its cousins'. The spines help the urchin move around or turn upright again after it has been flipped over, and some urchins have spines that sting as well.

Sea urchins usually eat seaweed, but they also eat bits of other plants and animals. Some are called sea eggs because of the shape of their bodies.

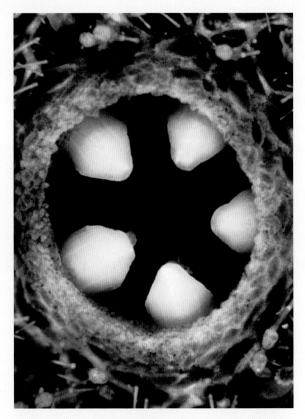

A sea urchin's five teeth are used for scraping, pulling, and tearing algae off hard surfaces. The teeth continue to grow throughout the urchins' life, so they are never worn down completely.

The red sea urchin *(below)* is one of the longest-living animals on Earth. Scientists have discovered red sea urchins up to two hundred years old! Many don't live that long. They may be eaten, die from diseases, or be harvested by humans. But the ones that survive show almost no sign of old age. They just keep growing very slowly. In fact, a one-hundred-year-old red sea urchin can still reproduce. And despite its age, it is as likely as a younger sea urchin to live another year.

One of the nicest souvenirs of a day at the beach is a sand dollar. The sand dollar is a type of sea urchin. It's a flat, circle-shaped creature that looks a little like a silver dollar made of sand.

You may find sand dollars on the sandy bottom of a tide pool or in the ocean itself.

When alive, most sand dollars have tube feet and short, bristling spines, which help them burrow in the sand.

When a sand dollar dies, it loses its bristles and tube feet and feels like sandpaper to the touch. You can find shells of dead sand dollars on the beach.

Above: **This sand dollar colony lives on the sandy bottom of the Pacific Ocean. Live sand dollars like these have bristles and tube feet covering their bodies.**
Inset: **When sand dollars die, they lose their bristles and tube feet as well as their color.**

A sea cucumber off the coast of Indonesia

SEA CUCUMBERS

When is a cucumber not a cucumber? When it's a sea cucumber, of course. These animals are another cousin of the starfish, although they look quite different.

Sea cucumbers live in all oceans in either deep or shallow water or in tide pools. They usually range in length from 2 to 18 inches (5–45 cm), but some are under 1 inch (2.5 cm), and others have been measured at 3 feet (90 cm) and longer.

When a sea cucumber is disturbed, it curls up into a ball. Some species can also spit out sticky threads.

If the water gets very shallow, some cucumbers can curl up into a ball to protect themselves from being dried out by the sun. When the water returns, the cucumber relaxes, stretches out, and shows off the ring of **tentacles** around its mouth. Sometimes the cucumber dries out in the process of stretching. Then it looks like a brittle piece of seaweed. But the tidewater will revive it.

Sea cucumbers often burrow into the wet sand. They swallow a lot of sand in the process, digesting the **organic material** (bits of other animals and plants) and eliminating the rest. In this way, they act very much as earthworms do on land.

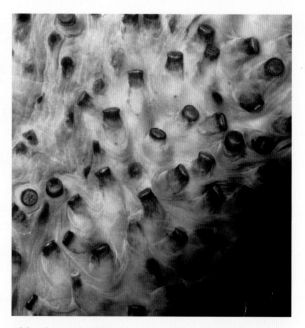

This close-up shows a warty sea cucumber's tube feet.

This sea cucumber has 10 feeding arms, or tentacles. One of the arms is in its mouth.

Above: This colorful grouping of sponges and sea squirts is found in Borneo, an island in Southeast Asia. *Opposite:* This type of sponge can be harvested and used around the house.

A Sea
of Life

TIDE POOLS AND SHALLOW WATERS ARE ALSO HOME TO many creatures that belong to other animal or plant groups. Some stay planted in one place. Some swim gracefully. Others crawl around the seafloor, exposed rocks, or sandy beaches. They eat differently and are built for sea life in diverse ways. But all thrive along coastlines around the world.

SPONGES
Most household sponges are made from synthetic materials. But some household sponges were once animals. Only certain animal sponges can become household sponges, though. Many are too prickly.

Saltwater sponges are animals filled with holes and **channels**. They have no heads, mouths, stomachs, or any other internal organs. Water flows right through them. Sponges take their food from this flowing water.

Living sea sponges are chock-full of **bacteria**. These single-celled organisms can make up more than half a sponge's weight! But a sponge's bacteria don't harm it. They help the sponge stay healthy, in exchange for a place to live. Scientists think the bacteria make compounds (chemicals) that could be used in medicine. Some scientists are trying to grow more of these bacteria to study this possibility.

This close-up shows the channels that gather water from within a sponge's body before it is pumped out the hole.

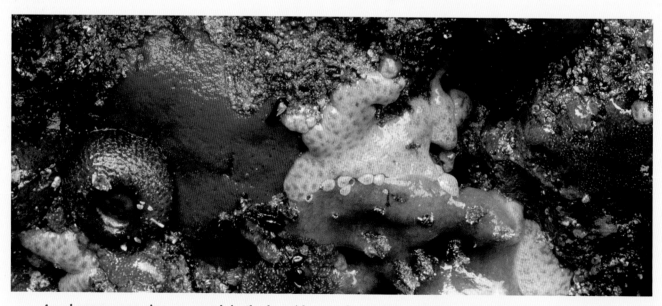

A red sponge growing on a rock in the low-tide zone is uncovered briefly when the water is lowest.

Above: **This sponge is found in tide pools in the Indo-Pacific oceans.**
Right: **A diver stops inside a giant barrel sponge in deeper ocean water.**

Sponges 1 to 4 inches (2.5–10 cm) tall can live on the floors and sides of tide pools. You'll find much larger sponges living farther out in the ocean, but the sponges in shallow water are often more colorful, and in the tropics, those colors may be even more intense.

You'll find sponges all over the world, but natural household sponges come mostly from the eastern half of the Mediterranean and waters near Mexico and the Bahamas.

Light bulb sea squirts live in groups in a jellylike mass. This species grows in the Mediterranean.

SEA SQUIRTS

Do sea squirts squirt? Touch one and find out! It just might spray you with a stream of water. The sea squirt contracts when it is disturbed and sends out a spray of water through one of its tubes, called siphons. These siphons are more often used to obtain food and eliminate waste. The sea squirt draws in water through one of its two siphons, strains it across gill slits where organic food is trapped, and lets the rest out through its other siphon.

When the sea squirt hatches from its

egg, it looks a lot like a tadpole. It has a tail and swims freely. But it changes shape as it grows. An adult looks like a plump bag with two tubes coming out of it. It no longer swims. Instead, it stays in one place, attached to seaweed, rocks, or wharf pilings.

Scientists call sea squirts **chordates** because of the tadpolelike stage in their early growth. Humans are chordates also. We, too, looked like tadpoles for a short time before we were born.

Sea squirts can be found all over the world, sometimes attached to the bottoms of ships, but most prefer shallow water.

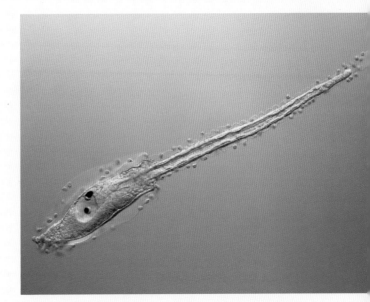

A sea squirt seen in its "tadpole" stage, magnified through a microscope

This blue translucent sea squirt (blue) and an ink spot sea squirt (white and purple) live in the waters off Borneo.

33

A white speckled hermit crab from the Caribbean Sea

HERMIT CRABS

A hermit crab lives in the empty shell of a dead snail. It will take over the shell of a dead snail, or it may drag a dying snail out of its shell and have the snail for lunch before making itself at home.

The hermit steals shells for homes because, unlike other crabs, it has soft, unprotected rear parts. It forms its soft body to the spiral inside the snail shell, and when threatened, it can draw itself entirely inside, using its tough claws like a door to seal the shell's opening.

Hermit crabs are found in oceans and on beaches all over the world. During low tide, you can find them on the floors of tide pools. Others cluster together on the ocean floor. Still others live on land, and some of these even climb into trees.

An Acadian hermit crab has left its shell to find a larger home.

A land hermit crab searches for a bigger shell.

JELLYFISH

If you walk along the beach, sometime you may see a jellylike mass. It is probably a jellyfish.

A jellyfish has a fragile inner and outer body wall. Contained between these two walls is the jellylike material that makes up this animal's soft skeleton and gives it its name.

A jellyfish swims by opening its body like an umbrella then quickly closing it again, thus pushing water out from underneath its body. This rapidly repeated action, or **jet propulsion**, pushes the animal upward or forward. When it stops swimming, it begins to sink, catching the tiny animals that it dines on as it comes down on top of them.

Above: **This blob on the beach is a dead jellyfish. Because jellyfish have soft skeletons, they do not keep their shape on land.**
Right: **The Crambione mastigophora is native to Thailand. This jellyfish has a crab and some fish in its bell.**

Jellyfish can sting, and because of this, some jellyfish are very dangerous. One kind, called the sea wasp, has a poison more deadly than that of any poisonous snake. Sea wasps live in coastal waters near northern Australia and the Philippines.

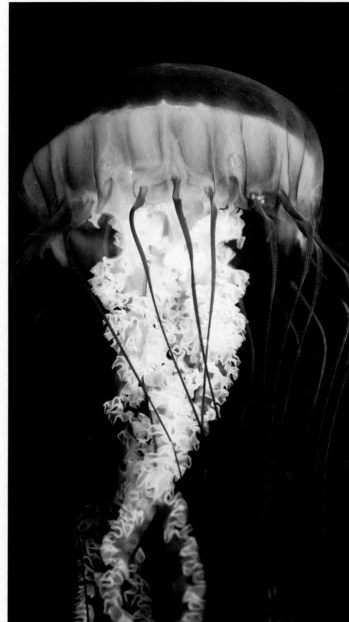

The Pacific Sea nettle jellyfish has 24 long, reddish, stinging tentacles.

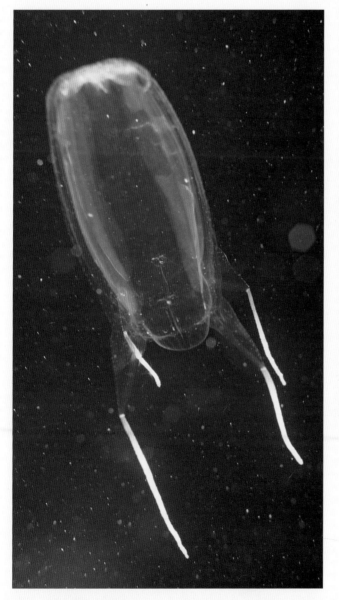

This sea wasp lives off the coast of Hawaii. Sea wasps are one of the most poisonous types of jellyfish.

Many jellyfish prefer warm, tropical waters, but you can also find jellyfish on British and U.S. shores. The jellyfish you see washed up on the shore most likely have died. However, they should not be handled because some can still sting.

This tide pool in California is home to many plants and animals, including green turf algae and marine snails.

ALGAE

One of the most common sights at the shore is seaweed. Most of the common saltwater plants we know as seaweed are kinds of algae. The tide brings them to shore.

Seaweed is very important to sea creatures. Many animals find shelter from the sun by hiding in patches of it. Some take on the color of the seaweed and so are well hidden from attackers. Other animals feed on seaweed.

Seaweed can be useful to people too. We get iodine from kelp, a brown seaweed, as well as a substance called algin. Algin is used in making ice cream. It keeps the water in the milk from making ice crystals when the ice cream is frozen. You can also find algin in salad dressings, chocolate milk, and aspirin.

A red seaweed called Irish moss, or carrageen, comes from Ireland, France, New England, and Canada. It's used in soups, desserts, and jams.

The Japanese prepare seaweed to eat by itself. This food, called nori, is usually made with a red seaweed that helps digestion.

These sushi rolls are wrapped in nori, or seaweed.

The country of Ireland has a new idea for the seaweed that grows near its shores. It wants to turn the seaweed into fuel. Bioethanol fuel is an alternative to fossil fuels such as coal, oil, and natural gas. Burning it may be better for the environment than burning fossil fuels. Bioethanol can already be made from plants such as corn and sugarcane, and brown seaweed is being investigated as another possible source. Someday seaweed may help to power the modern world!

A Fragile Balance

IF YOU HAVE BEEN TO AN OCEAN, YOU KNOW HOW BIG AND exciting it is. Maybe you have collected shells washed onto the shore and met some tide pool animals already. If you haven't been to an ocean yet, a wonderful experience is waiting for you.

However, you must be careful when visiting coastal areas. Many of the animals and plants at home there are easily harmed. They may get damaged when people step on them, pick them up out of the water, or even just touch them.

Human activities can disrupt the lives of coastal animals in other ways too. Oil spills from ships can wipe out large areas of ocean life. Pollution in the ocean from chemicals or trash can make the water unhealthy. Pollution and gases in the air are also trapping more of the sun's heat close to Earth, causing ocean temperatures to rise. Some creatures can't survive if the water gets too warm.

Life in tide pools has a careful balance. Animals rely on other animals and plants for food. If many clams in one area died out, for example, the starfish there might starve if they couldn't find enough other food. Then animals that feed on starfish might go hungry too. People must take steps to avoid upsetting that balance. When you venture to tide pools, remember that they are home to all these fascinating, fragile creatures. Take care so that future visitors can experience what you have—pools brimming with life.

Let the water cool your bare toes. Feel the wind blow through your hair as the sun warms your body. You are at the edge of the ocean and adventure awaits.

A family explores a tide pool on the coast of Southern California. People have to be careful when they explore tide pools so that they do not harm the creatures that live in them.

A Note about Scientific Classification

Are elephants, skunks, and sea cucumbers all in the same scientific group? You bet! They all belong in the animal kingdom, one of the largest groups. This keeps them separate from petunias, oak trees, and corn, all of which belong in the plant kingdom, another of the largest groups. These kingdoms are the first and largest groups in a system known as scientific classification.

In all, scientific classification includes seven chief groups. These are, from the largest to the smallest: (1) kingdom, (2) phylum or division, (3) class, (4) order, (5) family, (6) genus, and (7) species. A kingdom has many very different kinds of members in it. In a phylum, the members all become more alike, and so on down to the species, in which the members are all very much alike.

The following classifications show some of the larger scientific groups within which all the organisms in this book belong. These words may seem strange at first because, like all scientific names, they are in either Greek or Latin. This is so that scientists all over the world, whether they speak Chinese, English, or Arabic, can understand the same word for a plant or animal.

A tide pool in California

Animal Kingdom

Snail: Phylum: Mollusca
                   Class: Gastropoda

Periwinkle: Phylum: Mollusca
                   Class: Gastropoda
                   Family: Littorinidae

Clam: Phylum: Mollusca
                   Class: Bivalvia

Starfish: Phylum: Echinodermata
                   Class: Asteroidea

Brittle star: Phylum: Echinodermata
                   Class: Ophiuroidea

Sea urchin: Phylum: Echinodermata
                   Class: Echinoidea

Sand dollar: Phylum: Echinodermata
                   Class: Echinoidea

Sea cucumber: Phylum: Echinodermata
                   Class: Holothuroidea

Sponge: Phylum: Porifera

Sea squirt: Phylum: Chordata
                   Class: Ascidiacea

Hermit crab: Phylum: Arthropoda
                   Class: Crustacea
                   Family: Paguridae

Jellyfish: Phylum: Cnidaria
                   Class: Scyphozoa

Protista Kingdom*
Seaweed

Green alga: Division: Chlorophyta
Brown alga: Division: Phaeophyta
Red alga: Division: Rhodophyta

*Although seaweed is often called a plant, its body is built differently from true plants. Scientists classify it in the kingdom Protista.

Red algae

GLOSSARY

algae: a plant-like organism without roots or stems. Algae often form a filmy surface on rocks or grow as seaweed.

bacteria: tiny single-celled organisms. Some bacteria live inside sea creatures and help keep the host healthy in exchange for a place to live. Bacteria can also cause disease.

bivalves: creatures that have two shells hinged together in one place. Clams, oysters, and mussels are bivalves.

burrowing: digging a tunnel in the ground and taking shelter in it

channels: enclosed passages. In sponges, channels allow water to flow through the sponge, bringing tiny bits of food with it.

chordates: a group of animals that resemble tadpoles at some early stage of life. Humans and sea squirts are both chordates.

echinoderms: a group of animals that have spiny skin and often have five arms of equal size and shape or another five-point body design

eyespot: an eyelike spot that can sense light and dark

high tide: the highest level of the surface of the ocean, occurring twice each day. At high tide, water covers parts of beaches and tide pools are completely underwater.

jet propulsion: a way of moving by pushing water in the direction opposite where the body wants to go. Jellyfish use jet propulsion, pushing water down or back, to swim up or forward.

low tide: the lowest level of the surface of the ocean, occurring twice each day. At low tide, tide pools form and beaches have more area exposed.

mollusks: a group of animals with soft bodies, often protected by a hard shell

organic material: material made up of bits of dead plants and animals

rays: arms of a starfish

siphons: tubes that carry water in and out of some mollusks and other sea creatures

tentacles: flexible limbs used for moving, feeling, or grabbing. Snails and sea cucumbers have tentacles, as do the octopus and squid.

tide: the daily rise and fall of sea level, caused by the moon's gravitational pull and Earth's rotation

tide pool: a small pool filled with ocean water that was left behind when the tide went out. Tide pools are found mostly on rocky coasts.

tube feet: tube-shaped parts of echinoderms used for moving around or grabbing things. Tube feet often have suction cups at their ends to stick to surfaces.

SELECTED BIBLIOGRAPHY

AFP. "Seaweed Power: Ireland Taps New Energy Source." *Discovery Channel*. June 23, 2008. http://dsc.discovery.com/news/2008/06/23/ireland-seaweed-ethanol.html (October 20, 2008).

"Bacteria From Sponges Make New Pharmaceuticals." *ScienceDaily*. September 7, 2007. http://www.sciencedaily.com/releases/2007/09/070903204947.htm (October 20, 2008).

Barnard, Jeff. "Scientists: Warming Triggers 'Dead Zone.'" *USA Today*. July 27, 2006. http://www.usatoday.com/weather/climate/2006-07-27-dead-zone_x.htm (October 20, 2008).

Carson, Rachel. *The Edge of the Sea*. Boston: Houghton Mifflin, 1955.

Larousse Encyclopedia of Animal Life. London: Hamlyn, 1967.

Whitehouse, David. "Red Sea Urchin 'Almost Immortal.'" *BBC News*. November 24, 2003. http://news.bbc.co.uk/1/hi/sci/tech/3232002.stm (October 20, 2008).

WEBSITES

Habitats—Tidepool
http://olympiccoast.noaa.gov/living/habitats/tidepool/welcome.html
Click on the small pictures on this Web page to see great photos of tide pool life. Then follow the Living Sanctuary link to learn about different habitats and creatures of the Olympic Coast National Marine Sanctuary in Washington.

Monterey Bay Aquarium: Fun & Learning
http://www.mbayaq.org/lc/kids_place/
The Monterey Bay Aquarium's website includes information about sea creatures, journals from ocean explorers, a page on ocean science careers, and games and activities. You can even watch live webcam video of ocean life or send an electronic postcard.

Nature: Life at the Edge of the Sea
http://www.pbs.org/wnet/nature/edgeofsea/index.html
This website from the PBS show *Nature* includes features on tide pool life, the interaction of land and sea animals at coastlines, and filming underwater. Check out the virtual tide pool, where you can get a 360-degree view at high tide and at low tide.

NOAA Ocean Service Education

http://oceanservice.noaa.gov/education/welcome.html

On this website from the U.S. government's organization for ocean study, older students can read about recent ocean research and topics such as tides and pollution. Mapping activities are included for younger readers.

OLogy—Marine Biology: The Living Oceans

http://www.amnh.org/ology/?channel=marinebiology#

Choose among games, activities, quizzes, interviews, experiments, and articles that all will help you learn more about ocean life.

FURTHER READING

Bredeson, Carmen. *Tide Pools*. New York: Franklin Watts, 1999.

Connor, Judith. *Seashore Life on Rocky Coasts*. Monterey, CA: Monterey Bay Aquarium, 1993.

Fox, Sue. *Hermit Crabs*. New York: Barron's, 2000.

Hansen, Judith. *Seashells in My Pocket: AMC's Family Guide to Exploring the Coast from Maine to Florida*. Boston: Appalachian Mountain Club Books, 2008.

Johnson, Rebecca L. *A Journey into the Ocean*. Minneapolis: Carolrhoda Books, 2004.

Mallory, Kenneth. *A Home by the Sea: Protecting Coastal Wildlife*. San Diego: Harcourt Brace, 1998.

McKenzie, Michelle. *Jellyfish Inside Out*. Monterey, CA: Monterey Bay Aquarium, 2003.

INDEX

ABOUT THE AUTHOR

After spending 10 years in New York as a children's book editor and author, Anita Malnig moved to San Francisco, California. She became a founding editor for a children's computer magazine and later served as editorial director at Ziff-Davis's *MacWEEK*, communications manager at Apple Computer, and director of Web Site Services at Netopia, Inc. More recently, Malnig received a master's degree in English at San Francisco State University. She divides her time between writing articles on high-tech developments in publishing, consulting on public relations, and teaching composition and grammar at San Francisco State University. She has authored over 60 articles, columns, and books.

PHOTO ACKNOWLEDGMENTS

The images in this book are used with the permission of: © Daniel Gotshall/Visuals Unlimited/Getty Images, all backgrounds; © iStockphoto.com/Robert Plotz, pp. 2–3, 4; © Carol Hinz, pp. 5, 40; © Ken Lucas/Visuals Unlimited, Inc., pp. 6, 7 (bottom), 24 (main); © Laura Westlund/Independent Picture Service, pp. 7 (top), 9; © Jamie & Judy Wild/DanitaDelimont.com, p. 8; © iStockphoto.com/Nancy Nehring, p. 10; © Christophe Courteau/naturepl.com, p. 11; © Gerald & Buff Corsi/Visuals Unlimited, Inc., pp. 12, 38, © Gary K. Smith/naturepl.com, p. 13; © Gary G. Gibson/Photo Researchers, Inc., p. 14 (top); © Andrew J. Martinez/Photo Researchers, Inc., p. 15 (top); © Richard Hermann/Visuals Unlimited, Inc., pp. 15 (bottom), 42; © Ian McAllister/All Canada Photos/Getty Images, p. 16; © iStockphoto .com/Andrew Helwich, p. 17; © Reinhard Dirscherl/Visuals Unlimited, Inc., p. 18 (both); © Francis & Donna Caldwell/Visuals Unlimited, Inc., p. 19 (top); © Dwight Kuhn, pp. 19 (bottom), 22 (top), 35 (both); © Wim van Egmond/Visuals Unlimited, Inc., pp. 20, 33; © carlo greco/photosynthesis, p. 21; © Kjell Sandved/Visuals Unlimited, Inc., p. 22 (bottom); © Jeff Rotman/The Image Bank/Getty Images, p. 23; © Rich Reid/National Geographic/Getty Images, p. 24 (inset); © Norbert Wu/Science Faction/ Getty Images, pp. 25, 26 (top), 28; © David Wrobel/Visuals Unlimited, Inc., pp. 26 (bottom), 27; © WILDLIFE/Peter Arnold, Inc., p. 29; © Jeff Rotman/Iconica/Getty Images, pp. 30 (top), 31 (bottom); © Doug Sokell/Visuals Unlimited, Inc., p. 30 (bottom); © Jurgen Freund/naturepl.com, p. 31 (top); © age fotostock/SuperStock, p. 32; © Georgette Douwma/Photo Researchers, Inc., p. 33 (bottom); © Heather Perry/National Geographic/Getty Images, p. 34; © iStockphoto.com/Buretsu, p. 36 (main); © David Fleetham/Visuals Unlimited, Inc., pp. 36 (inset), 37 (left); © SMC Images/Photodisc/Getty Images, p. 37 (right); © Peter Gau/Dreamstime.com, p. 39 (bottom); © David Smith/Dreamstime.com, p. 39 (top); © Tom Uhlman/Alamy, p. 41; © Daniel Gotshall/Visuals Unlimited, Inc., p. 43.

Front cover: © Raymond K. Gehman/National Geographic/Getty Images.

Back cover: © Daniel Gotshall/Visuals Unlimited/Getty Images.